DOVER · THRIFT

"Easter 1916" and Other Poems

WILLIAM BUTLER YEATS

DOVER PUBLICATIONS, INC.
Mineola, New York

DOVER THRIFT EDITIONS

GENERAL EDITOR: PAUL NEGRI
EDITOR OF THIS VOLUME: JAMES REILLY

Bibliographical Note

This Dover edition, first published in 1997, is an unabridged republication of William Butler Yeats's poems from the volumes *The Wild Swans at Coole* and *Michael Robartes and the Dancer*, as published in *Later Poems* by Macmillan and Co., London, 1922. Slight alterations in punctuation have been made in a few instances, and an introductory Note and an Alphabetical List of Titles and First Lines have been specially prepared for the present edition.

Library of Congress Cataloging-in-Publication Data

Yeats, W. B. (William Butler), 1865–1939.
[Later poems]
"Easter 1916" and other poems / William Butler Yeats.
p.   cm. — (Dover thrift editions)
Originally published: Later poems, 1922.
ISBN 0-486-29771-3 (pbk.)
1. Ireland — Poetry.   I. Title   II. Series.
PR5904.L36   1997
821'.8 — dc21   97-25229
                                                      CIP

Manufactured in the United States of America
Dover Publications, Inc., 31 East 2nd Street, Mineola, N.Y. 11501

Note

In 1900, with perhaps a touch of melancholia understandable in a middle-aged bachelor-aesthete standing at the crossroads of two centuries, William Butler Yeats (1865–1939) observed that "a poet, or even a mystic, becomes a greater power from understanding all the great primary emotions and those one only gets out of going through the common experiences and duties of life." Seventeen years later, at the age of 52, the Irishman married for the first and only time and proceeded to transform his rather modest observation into a personal prophesy.

Indeed, it would be no exaggeration to suggest that, had he died instead of marrying in 1917 — had his life flamed only briefly, like those of the English Romantics Keats, Shelley, and Byron in whose tradition he began writing in the 1890s — Yeats would have likely been remembered as a minor poet who, despite the achievement of a distinctive diction, was capable of only occasional brilliance. Yet, in wedding Miss Georgie Hyde-Lees, the poet effectively abandoned his initially inspiring — and then only enervating — thirty-year pursuit of Maud Gonne, the beautiful and fiery Irish nationalist with whom he had fallen madly in love in 1889, and shed the aloofness and eccentricities of single living, becoming in marriage, as he described it, "more knitted to life." As significant as what he shed, however, was what he gained: new energies fueled by his wife's automatic writing, or her ability to suspend her conscious faculties to record dreams, fragmentary mental images, and even the dictations of dead spirits. The poet came to believe that Mrs. Yeats's ghostly scribblings, recorded in notebooks by husband and wife in two- and three-hour daily sessions, had at long last put wisdom within his reach and provided new metaphors for a poetic genre he well could have eventually neglected in favor of plays, essays, and public speaking.

The skeptic may question Yeats's peculiar methodology, but few dispute the quality of the verse it inspired, notably in four volumes appearing in the inter-war years. In *The Wild Swans at Coole* (1919) and *Michael Robartes and the Dancer* (1921) — offered here in their original entirety — and in *The Tower* (1928) and *The Winding Stair* (1933) may be found some of the finest poetry of this or, indeed, any century. In these groups of poems, strong rhythms and a sparsely embroidered diction undergird a combination of symbols (swan, tower, moon, etc.), each invested with a multiplicity of meanings considered quintessentially 'Yeatsian.' In the last twenty years of his life, Yeats had finally broken beyond the borders of his island-nation and cemented his reputation as an international poet of the first order. Herein are the early stirrings toward this eventual achievement.

"The Wild Swans at Coole," the first poem of the volume of the same name, is a crisp lyric on the mutability of life amid the seeming immutability of nature and was written while Yeats was living in his Thoor Ballylee tower near Coole Park, the Co. Galway estate of his longtime benefactress, Lady Augusta Gregory. And the connection to Lady Gregory continues, as the conversational "In Memory of Major Robert Gregory," the elegiac "An Irish Airman Foresees His Death," and the pastoral "The Sad Shepherd" all celebrate her son, a talented painter and skilled horseman killed in World War I.

Aging's torments are explored in "Men Improve with the Years," "The Living Beauty," "A Song," "Solomon to Sheba," "To a Young Beauty," and "To a Young Girl," the last two having been addressed to Maud Gonne's teenage daughter Iseult, to whom the poet once proposed marriage!

Yeats's ubiquitous 'noble beggar' appears in "Under the Round Tower" and reappears in the self-consciously wrought "The Fisherman," a kind of peasant aristocrat representing not only a vanished romantic Ireland but a poet lamenting its disappearance."

The consecutively arranged "Her Praise," "The People," "His Phoenix," "A Thought from Propertius," and "Broken Dreams" all more or less concern themselves with Maud Gonne, while the final few selections of *The Wild Swans at Coole* are colored by Yeats's developing theories of history and astrological character analysis, particularly as they reveal themselves in the paranormally inspired personae of Hic and Ille, Owen Aherne, and Michael Robartes, and the Saint and the Hunchback. In "Ego Dominus Tuus," "The Phases of the Moon," and "The Double Vision of Michael Robartes," full-throated Yeatsian mysticism emerges — and just in time to varnish Yeatsian politics in the subsequent *Michael Robartes and the Dancer*.

The brevity of the second volume of poems belies its significance, for *Michael Robartes and the Dancer* contains some of Yeats's most anthologized works. It was composed in the shadow of the nationalist Easter Uprising of 1916, released in the latter days of the Anglo-Irish War (1919–21) and read during the Irish Civil War (1922–23) and eventual establishment of the Irish Free State (1922), and therefore, unsurprisingly evidences a resurgence of the poet's love-hate interest in public matters. For in this period, Irish cultural and political nationalism, to which Yeats had strenuously devoted himself, largely symbolized by his work in establishing the Abbey Theater in Dublin, had been overtaken by armed nationalism. The street had supplanted the stage as the forum for Irish renewal, and in this milieu and in these writings, Yeats wrestled with the relevancy of art and its concessions to action.

In truth, this Protestant-born Anglo-Irish aristocrat had initially been indignant over the abortive 1916 Dublin insurrection (as had been many natives at the time), but soon found in it the appeal of 'the glorious failure,' immortalizing in "Easter 1916" heretofore ordinary souls — schoolteacher Patrick Pearse, Major John MacBride (a "drunken, vain-glorious lout" and one-time husband of Maud Gonne) and boyhood friend and fellow Co. Sligo native Constance Markiewicz, among others — for their heroic sacrifice at the hands of Ireland's British occupiers. And ever with one eye on the crowd and its posterity, Yeats sealed the canonization — theirs and, in some sense, his — with "Sixteen Dead Men," "The Rose Tree," and "On a Political Prisoner."

Despite the poet's renewed confidence in Irish national fortunes, however, a resigned morbidity about the future in general persisted. It is given a personal dimension in "A Prayer for My Daughter," and a foreboding darkness in "Demon and Beast," as well as arguably the poet's most famous poem, "The Second Coming," which ultimately defines the volume's tone and tenor.

A deeply religious man who found himself unable to assent to Christian doctrine, Yeats nonetheless exploited imagery supremely saleable in Catholic Ireland and the Christian West. In "The Second Coming," his conception of history as unfolding in two-thousand-year cycles, each inaugurated by a dramatic cosmological revelation, is versified in a thoroughly anti-modern eschatology: What kind of era will follow the pre-Christian and now-fading Christian epochs?

In 1923, two years after the release of "The Second Coming," William Butler Yeats was awarded the Nobel Prize for Literature, having already been invited to join the Irish Free State Senate a year earlier — testaments to two of his finest attributes: his skill at matching intensity of emotion with fully crafted art — vision with virtuosity — and his sensitivity to the dynamic by which art fires, and in turn is fired by, the public imagination.

Contents

From *Michael Robartes and the Dancer*, 1921

THE WILD SWANS AT COOLE

The trees are in their autumn beauty,
The woodland paths are dry,
Under the October twilight the water
Mirrors a still sky;
Upon the brimming water among the stones
Are nine and fifty swans.

The nineteenth Autumn has come upon me
Since I first made my count;
I saw, before I had well finished,
All suddenly mount
And scatter wheeling in great broken rings
Upon their clamorous wings.

I have looked upon those brilliant creatures,
And now my heart is sore.
All's changed since I, hearing at twilight,
The first time on this shore,
The bell-beat of their wings above my head,
Trod with a lighter tread.

Unwearied still, lover by lover,
They paddle in the cold,
Companionable streams or climb the air;
Their hearts have not grown old;
Passion or conquest, wander where they will,
Attend upon them still.

But now they drift on the still water
Mysterious, beautiful;
Among what rushes will they build,

By what lake's edge or pool
Delight men's eyes when I awake some day
To find they have flown away?

IN MEMORY OF MAJOR ROBERT GREGORY

I

Now that we're almost settled in our house
I'll name the friends that cannot sup with us
Beside a fire of turf in th' ancient tower,
And having talked to some late hour
Climb up the narrow winding stair to bed:
Discoverers of forgotten truth
Or mere companions of my youth,
All, all are in my thoughts to-night being dead.

II

Always we'd have the new friend meet the old
And we are hurt if either friend seem cold,
And there is salt to lengthen out the smart
In the affections of our heart,
And quarrels are blown up upon that head;
But not a friend that I would bring
This night can set us quarrelling,
For all that come into my mind are dead.

III

Lionel Johnson comes the first to mind,
That loved his learning better than mankind,
Though courteous to the worst; much falling he
Brooded upon sanctity
Till all his Greek and Latin learning seemed
A long blast upon the horn that brought
A little nearer to his thought
A measureless consummation that he dreamed.

IV

And that enquiring man John Synge comes next
That dying chose the living world for text
And never could have rested in the tomb
But that, long travelling, he had come
Towards nightfall upon certain set apart
In a most desolate stony place,
Towards nightfall upon a race
Passionate and simple like his heart.

V

And then I think of old George Pollexfen,
In muscular youth well known to Mayo men
For horsemanship at meets or at racecourses,
That could have shown how purebred horses
And solid men, for all their passion, live
But as the outrageous stars incline
By opposition, square and trine;
Having grown sluggish and contemplative.

VI

They were my close companions many a year,
A portion of my mind and life, as it were,
And now their breathless faces seem to look
Out of some old picture-book;
I am accustomed to their lack of breath,
But not that my dear friend's dear son,
Our Sidney and our perfect man,
Could share in that discourtesy of death.

VII

For all things the delighted eye now sees
Were loved by him; the old storm-broken trees
That cast their shadows upon road and bridge;
The tower set on the stream's edge;

The ford where drinking cattle make a stir
Nightly, and startled by that sound
The water-hen must change her ground;
He might have been your heartiest welcomer.

VIII

When with the Galway foxhounds he would ride
From Castle Taylor to the Roxborough side
Or Esserkelly plain, few kept his pace;
At Mooneen he had leaped a place
So perilous that half the astonished meet
Had shut their eyes, and where was it
He rode a race without a bit?
And yet his mind outran the horses' feet.

IX

We dreamed that a great painter had been born
To cold Clare rock and Galway rock and thorn,
To that stern colour and that delicate line
That are our secret discipline
Wherein the gazing heart doubles her might.
Soldier, scholar, horseman, he,
And yet he had the intensity
To have published all to be a world's delight.

X

What other could so well have counselled us
In all lovely intricacies of a house
As he that practised or that understood
All work in metal or in wood,
In moulded plaster or in carven stone?
Soldier, scholar, horseman, he,
And all he did done perfectly
As though he had but that one trade alone.

XI

Some burn damp fagots, others may consume
The entire combustible world in one small room—
As though dried straw, and if we turn about
The bare chimney is gone black out
Because the work had finished in that flare.
Soldier, scholar, horseman, he,
As 'twere all life's epitome.
What made us dream that he could comb grey hair?

XII

I had thought, seeing how bitter is that wind
That shakes the shutter, to have brought to mind
All those that manhood tried, or childhood loved
Or boyish intellect approved,
With some appropriate commentary on each;
Until imagination brought
A fitter welcome; but a thought
Of that late death took all my heart for speech.

AN IRISH AIRMAN FORESEES HIS DEATH

I know that I shall meet my fate
Somewhere among the clouds above;
Those that I fight I do not hate,
Those that I guard I do not love;
My country is Kiltartan Cross,
My countrymen Kiltartan's poor,
No likely end could bring them loss
Or leave them happier than before.
Nor law, nor duty bade me fight,
Nor public men, nor cheering crowds,
A lonely impulse of delight
Drove to this tumult in the clouds;
I balanced all, brought all to mind,

The years to come seemed waste of breath,
A waste of breath the years behind
In balance with this life, this death.

MEN IMPROVE WITH THE YEARS

I am worn out with dreams;
A weather-worn, marble triton
Among the streams;
And all day long I look
Upon this lady's beauty
As though I had found in book
A pictured beauty,
Pleased to have filled the eyes
Or the discerning ears,
Delighted to be but wise,
For men improve with the years;
And yet and yet
Is this my dream, or the truth?
O would that we had met
When I had my burning youth;
But I grow old among dreams,
A weather-worn, marble triton
Among the streams.

THE COLLAR-BONE OF A HARE

Would I could cast a sail on the water
Where many a king has gone
And many a king's daughter,
And alight at the comely trees and the lawn,
The playing upon pipes and the dancing,
And learn that the best thing is
To change my loves while dancing
And pay but a kiss for a kiss.

I would find by the edge of that water
The collar-bone of a hare
Worn thin by the lapping of water,
And pierce it through with a gimlet and stare
At the old bitter world where they marry in churches,
And laugh over the untroubled water
At all who marry in churches,
Through the white thin bone of a hare.

UNDER THE ROUND TOWER

"Although I'd lie lapped up in linen
A deal I'd sweat and little earn
If I should live as live the neighbours,"
Cried the beggar, Billy Byrne;
"Stretch bones till the daylight come
On great-grandfather's battered tomb."

Upon a grey old battered tombstone
In Glendalough beside the stream,
Where the O'Byrnes and Byrnes are buried,
He stretched his bones and fell in a dream
Of sun and moon that a good hour
Bellowed and pranced in the round tower;

Of golden king and silver lady,
Bellowing up and bellowing round,
Till toes mastered a sweet measure,
Mouth mastered a sweet sound,
Prancing round and prancing up
Until they pranced upon the top.

That golden king and that wild lady
Sang till stars began to fade,
Hands gripped in hands, toes close together,
Hair spread on the wind they made;
That lady and that golden king
Could like a brace of blackbirds sing.

"It's certain that my luck is broken,"
That rambling jailbird Billy said;
"Before nightfall I'll pick a pocket
And snug it in a feather-bed,
I cannot find the peace of home
On great-grandfather's battered tomb."

SOLOMON TO SHEBA

Sang Solomon to Sheba,
And kissed her dusky face,
"All day long from mid-day
We have talked in the one place,
All day long from shadowless noon
We have gone round and round
In the narrow theme of love
Like an old horse in a pound."

To Solomon sang Sheba,
Planted on his knees,
"If you had broached a matter
That might the learned please,
You had before the sun had thrown
Our shadows on the ground
Discovered that my thoughts, not it,
Are but a narrow pound."

Sang Solomon to Sheba,
And kissed her Arab eyes,
"There's not a man or woman
Born under the skies
Dare match in learning with us two,
And all day long we have found
There's not a thing but love can make
The world a narrow pound."

THE LIVING BEAUTY

I'll say and maybe dream I have drawn content —
Seeing that time has frozen up the blood,
The wick of youth being burned and the oil spent —
From beauty that is cast out of a mould
In bronze, or that in dazzling marble appears,
Appears, and when we have gone is gone again,
Being more indifferent to our solitude
Than 'twere an apparition. O heart, we are old,
The living beauty is for younger men,
We cannot pay its tribute of wild tears.

A SONG

I thought no more was needed
Youth to prolong
Than dumb-bell and foil
To keep the body young.
Oh, who could have foretold
That the heart grows old?

Though I have many words,
What woman's satisfied,
I am no longer faint
Because at her side?
Oh, who could have foretold
That the heart grows old?

I have not lost desire
But the heart that I had;
I thought 'twould burn my body
Laid on the death-bed,
For who could have foretold
That the heart grows old?

TO A YOUNG BEAUTY

Dear fellow-artist, why so free
With every sort of company,
With every Jack and Jill?
Choose your companions from the best;
Who draws a bucket with the rest
Soon topples down the hill.

You may, that mirror for a school,
Be passionate, not bountiful
As common beauties may,
Who were not born to keep in trim
With old Ezekiel's cherubim
But those of Beaujolet.

I know what wages beauty gives,
How hard a life her servant lives,
Yet praise the winters gone:
There is not a fool can call me friend,
And I may dine at journey's end
With Landor and with Donne.

TO A YOUNG GIRL

My dear, my dear, I know
More than another
What makes your heart beat so;
Not even your own mother
Can know it as I know,
Who broke my heart for her
When the wild thought,
That she denies
And has forgot,
Set all her blood astir
And glittered in her eyes.

THE SCHOLARS

Bald heads forgetful of their sins,
Old, learned, respectable bald heads
Edit and annotate the lines
That young men, tossing on their beds,
Rhymed out in love's despair
To flatter beauty's ignorant ear.

They'll cough in the ink to the world's end;
Wear out the carpet with their shoes
Earning respect; have no strange friend;
If they have sinned nobody knows.
Lord, what would they say
Should their Catullus walk that way?

TOM O'ROUGHLEY

"Though logic choppers rule the town,
And every man and maid and boy
Has marked a distant object down,
An aimless joy is a pure joy,"
Or so did Tom O'Roughley say
That saw the surges running by,
"And wisdom is a butterfly
And not a gloomy bird of prey.

"If little planned is little sinned
But little need the grave distress.
What's dying but a second wind?
How but in zig-zag wantonness
Could trumpeter Michael be so brave?"
Or something of that sort he said,
"And if my dearest friend were dead
I'd dance a measure on his grave."

SHEPHERD AND GOATHERD

SHEPHERD

That cry's from the first cuckoo of the year.
I wished before it ceased.

GOATHERD

                    Nor bird nor beast
Could make me wish for anything this day,
Being old, but that the old alone might die,
And that would be against God's Providence.
Let the young wish. But what has brought you here?
Never until this moment have we met
Where my goats browse on the scarce grass or leap
From stone to stone.

SHEPHERD

                    I am looking for strayed sheep;
Something has troubled me and in my trouble
I let them stray. I thought of rhyme alone,
For rhyme can beat a measure out of trouble
And make the daylight sweet once more; but when
I had driven every rhyme into its place
The sheep had gone from theirs.

GOATHERD

                    I know right well
What turned so good a shepherd from his charge.

SHEPHERD

He that was best in every country sport
And every country craft, and of us all
Most courteous to slow age and hasty youth,
Is dead.

GOATHERD

The boy that brings my griddle cake
Brought the bare news.

SHEPHERD

He had thrown the crook away
And died in the great war beyond the sea.

GOATHERD

He had often played his pipes among my hills,
And when he played it was their loneliness,
The exultation of their stone, that cried
Under his fingers.

SHEPHERD

I had it from his mother,
And his own flock was browsing at the door.

GOATHERD

How does she bear her grief? There is not a shepherd
But grows more gentle when he speaks her name,
Remembering kindness done, and how can I,
That found when I had neither goat nor grazing
New welcome and old wisdom at her fire
Till winter blasts were gone, but speak of her
Even before his children and his wife.

SHEPHERD

She goes about her house erect and calm
Between the pantry and the linen chest,
Or else at meadow or at grazing overlooks
Her labouring men, as though her darling lived,
But for her grandson now; there is no change
But such as I have seen upon her face

Watching our shepherd sports at harvest-time
When her son's turn was over.

GOATHERD

Sing your song,
I too have rhymed my reveries, but youth
Is hot to show whatever it has found,
And till that's done can neither work nor wait.
Old goatherds and old goats, if in all else
Youth can excel them in accomplishment,
Are learned in waiting.

SHEPHERD

You cannot but have seen
That he alone had gathered up no gear,
Set carpenters to work on no wide table,
On no long bench nor lofty milking shed
As others will, when first they take possession,
But left the house as in his father's time
As though he knew himself, as it were, a cuckoo,
No settled man. And now that he is gone
There's nothing of him left but half a score
Of sorrowful, austere, sweet, lofty pipe tunes.

GOATHERD

You have put the thought in rhyme.

SHEPHERD

I worked all day,
And when 'twas done so little had I done
That maybe "I am sorry" in plain prose
Had sounded better to your mountain fancy.
                                    [*He sings.*]
"Like the speckled bird that steers
Thousands of leagues oversea,

And runs for a while or a while half-flies
Upon his yellow legs through our meadows,
He stayed for a while; and we
Had scarcely accustomed our ears
To his speech at the break of day,
Had scarcely accustomed our eyes
To his shape at the rinsing pool
Among the evening shadows,
When he vanished from ears and eyes.
I had wished a dear thing on that day
I heard him first, but man is a fool."

GOATHERD

You sing as always of the natural life,
And I that made like music in my youth
Hearing it now have sighed for that young man
And certain lost companions of my own.

SHEPHERD

They say that on your barren mountain ridge
You have measured out the road that the soul treads
When it has vanished from our natural eyes;
That you have talked with apparitions.

GOATHERD

                                         Indeed
My daily thoughts since the first stupor of youth
Have found the path my goats' feet cannot find.

SHEPHERD

Sing, for it may be that your thoughts have plucked
Some medicable herb to make our grief
Less bitter.

GOATHERD

They have brought me from that ridge
Seed pods and flowers that are not all wild poppy.
[*Sings*.]
"He grows younger every second
That were all his birthdays reckoned
Much too solemn seemed;
Because of what he had dreamed,
Or the ambitions that he served,
Much too solemn and reserved.
Jaunting, journeying
To his own dayspring,
He unpacks the loaded pern
Of all 'twas pain or joy to learn,
Of all that he had made.
The outrageous war shall fade;
At some old winding whitethorn root
He'll practise on the shepherd's flute,
Or on the close-cropped grass
Court his shepherd lass,
Or run where lads reform our daytime
Till that is their long shouting playtime;
Knowledge he shall unwind
Through victories of the mind,
Till, clambering at the cradle side,
He dreams himself his mother's pride,
All knowledge lost in trance
Of sweeter ignorance."

SHEPHERD

When I have shut these ewes and this old ram
Into the fold, we'll to the woods and there
Cut out our rhymes on strips of new-torn bark
But put no name and leave them at her door.
To know the mountain and the valley have grieved
May be a quiet thought to wife and mother,
And children when they spring up shoulder high.

LINES WRITTEN IN DEJECTION

When have I last looked on
The round green eyes and the long wavering bodies
Of the dark leopards of the moon?
All the wild witches those most noble ladies,
For all their broom-sticks and their tears,
Their angry tears, are gone.
The holy centaurs of the hills are vanished;
I have nothing but the embittered sun;
Banished heroic mother moon and vanished,
And now that I have come to fifty years
I must endure the timid sun.

THE DAWN

I would be ignorant as the dawn
That has looked down
On that old queen measuring a town
With the pin of a brooch,
Or on the withered men that saw
From their pedantic Babylon
The careless planets in their courses,
The stars fade out where the moon comes,
And took their tablets and did sums;
I would be ignorant as the dawn
That merely stood, rocking the glittering coach
Above the cloudy shoulders of the horses;
I would be — for no knowledge is worth a straw —
Ignorant and wanton as the dawn.

ON WOMAN

May God be praised for woman
That gives up all her mind,
A man may find in no man
A friendship of her kind
That covers all he has brought
As with her flesh and bone,
Nor quarrels with a thought
Because it is not her own.

Though pedantry denies
It's plain the Bible means
That Solomon grew wise
While talking with his queens.
Yet never could, although
They say he counted grass,
Count all the praises due
When Sheba was his lass,
When she the iron wrought, or
When from the smithy fire
It shuddered in the water:
Harshness of their desire
That made them stretch and yawn,
Pleasure that comes with sleep,
Shudder that made them one.
What else He give or keep
God grant me — no, not here,
For I am not so bold
To hope a thing so dear
Now I am growing old,
But when if the tale's true
The Pestle of the moon
That pounds up all anew
Brings me to birth again —
To find what once I had
And know what once I have known,
Until I am driven mad,

Sleep driven from my bed,
By tenderness and care,
Pity, an aching head,
Gnashing of teeth, despair;
And all because of some one
Perverse creature of chance,
And live like Solomon
That Sheba led a dance.

THE FISHERMAN

Although I can see him still,
The freckled man who goes
To a grey place on a hill
In grey Connemara clothes
At dawn to cast his flies,
It's long since I began
To call up to the eyes
This wise and simple man.
All day I'd looked in the face
What I had hoped 'twould be
To write for my own race
And the reality;
The living men that I hate,
The dead man that I loved,
The craven man in his seat,
The insolent unreproved,
And no knave brought to book
Who has won a drunken cheer,
The witty man and his joke
Aimed at the commonest ear,
The clever man who cries
The catch-cries of the clown,
The beating down of the wise
And great Art beaten down.

Maybe a twelvemonth since
Suddenly I began,

In scorn of this audience,
Imagining a man,
And his sun-freckled face,
And grey Connemara cloth,
Climbing up to a place
Where stone is dark under froth,
And the down turn of his wrist
When the flies drop in the stream;
A man who does not exist,
A man who is but a dream;
And cried, "Before I am old
I shall have written him one
Poem maybe as cold
And passionate as the dawn."

THE HAWK

"Call down the hawk from the air;
Let him be hooded or caged
Till the yellow eye has grown mild,
For larder and spit are bare,
The old cook enraged,
The scullion gone wild."

"I will not be clapped in a hood,
Nor a cage, nor alight upon wrist,
Now I have learnt to be proud
Hovering over the wood
In the broken mist
Or tumbling cloud."

"What tumbling cloud did you cleave,
Yellow-eyed hawk of the mind,
Last evening? that I, who had sat
Dumbfounded before a knave,
Should give to my friend
A pretence of wit."

MEMORY

One had a lovely face,
And two or three had charm,
But charm and face were in vain
Because the mountain grass
Cannot but keep the form
Where the mountain hare has lain.

HER PRAISE

She is foremost of those that I would hear praised.
I have gone about the house, gone up and down
As a man does who has published a new book
Or a young girl dressed out in her new gown,
And though I have turned the talk by hook or crook
Until her praise should be the uppermost theme,
A woman spoke of some new tale she had read,
A man confusedly in a half dream
As though some other name ran in his head.
She is foremost of those that I would hear praised.
I will talk no more of books or the long war
But walk by the dry thorn until I have found
Some beggar sheltering from the wind, and there
Manage the talk until her name come round.
If there be rags enough he will know her name
And be well pleased remembering it, for in the old days,
Though she had young men's praise and old men's blame,
Among the poor both old and young gave her praise.

THE PEOPLE

"What have I earned for all that work," I said,
"For all that I have done at my own charge?
The daily spite of this unmannerly town,
Where who has served the most is most defamed,
The reputation of his lifetime lost
Between the night and morning. I might have lived,
And you know well how great the longing has been,
Where every day my footfall should have lit
In the green shadow of Ferrara wall;
Or climbed among the images of the past —
The unperturbed and courtly images —
Evening and morning, the steep street of Urbino
To where the duchess and her people talked
The stately midnight through until they stood
In their great window looking at the dawn;
I might have had no friend that could not mix
Courtesy and passion into one like those
That saw the wicks grow yellow in the dawn;
I might have used the one substantial right
My trade allows: chosen my company,
And chosen what scenery had pleased me best."
Thereon my phoenix answered in reproof,
"The drunkards, pilferers of public funds,
All the dishonest crowd I had driven away,
When my luck changed and they dared meet my face,
Crawled from obscurity, and set upon me
Those I had served and some that I had fed;
Yet never have I, now nor any time,
Complained of the people."

                          All I could reply
Was: "You, that have not lived in thought but deed,
Can have the purity of a natural force,
But I, whose virtues are the definitions
Of the analytic mind, can neither close
The eye of the mind nor keep my tongue from speech."

And yet, because my heart leaped at her words,
I was abashed, and now they come to mind
After nine years, I sink my head abashed.

HIS PHOENIX

There is a queen in China, or maybe it's in Spain,
And birthdays and holidays such praises can be heard
Of her unblemished lineaments, a whiteness with no stain,
That she might be that sprightly girl who was trodden by a bird;
And there's a score of duchesses, surpassing womankind,
Or who have found a painter to make them so for pay
And smooth out stain and blemish with the elegance of his mind:
I knew a phoenix in my youth so let them have their day.

The young men every night applaud their Gaby's laughing eye,
And Ruth St. Denis had more charm although she had poor luck,
From nineteen hundred nine or ten, Pavlova's had the cry,
And there's a player in the States who gathers up her cloak
And flings herself out of the room when Juliet would be bride
With all a woman's passion, a child's imperious way,
And there are — but no matter if there are scores beside:
I knew a phoenix in my youth so let them have their day.

There's Margaret and Marjorie and Dorothy and Nan,
A Daphne and a Mary who live in privacy;
One's had her fill of lovers, another's had but one,
Another boasts, "I pick and choose and have but two or three."
If head and limb have beauty and the instep's high and light
They can spread out what sail they please for all I have to say,
Be but the breakers of men's hearts or engines of delight:
I knew a phoenix in my youth so let them have their day.

There'll be that crowd, that barbarous crowd, through all the centuries,
And who can say but some young belle may walk and talk men wild
Who is my beauty's equal, though that my heart denies,

But not the exact likeness, the simplicity of a child,
And that proud look as though she had gazed into the burning sun,
And all the shapely body no tittle gone astray.
I mourn for that most lonely thing; and yet God's will be done,
I knew a phoenix in my youth so let them have their day.

A THOUGHT FROM PROPERTIUS

She might, so noble from head
To great shapely knees
The long flowing line,
Have walked to the altar
Through the holy images
At Pallas Athene's side,
Or been fit spoil for a centaur
Drunk with the unmixed wine.

BROKEN DREAMS

There is grey in your hair.
Young men no longer suddenly catch their breath
When you are passing;
But maybe some old gaffer mutters a blessing
Because it was your prayer
Recovered him upon the bed of death.
For your sole sake — that all heart's ache have known,
And given to others all heart's ache,
From meagre girlhood's putting on
Burdensome beauty — for your sole sake
Heaven has put away the stroke of her doom,
So great her portion in that peace you make
By merely walking in a room.

Your beauty can but leave among us
Vague memories, nothing but memories.
A young man when the old men are done talking

Will say to an old man, "Tell me of that lady
The poet stubborn with his passion sang us
When age might well have chilled his blood."

Vague memories, nothing but memories,
But in the grave all, all, shall be renewed.
The certainty that I shall see that lady
Leaning or standing or walking
In the first loveliness of womanhood,
And with the fervour of my youthful eyes,
Has set me muttering like a fool.

You are more beautiful than any one
And yet your body had a flaw:
Your small hands were not beautiful,
And I am afraid that you will run
And paddle to the wrist
In that mysterious, always brimming lake
Where those that have obeyed the holy law
Paddle and are perfect; leave unchanged
The hands that I have kissed
For old sakes' sake.

The last stroke of midnight dies.
All day in the one chair
From dream to dream and rhyme to rhyme I have ranged
In rambling talk with an image of air:
Vague memories, nothing but memories.

A DEEP-SWORN VOW

Others because you did not keep
That deep-sworn vow have been friends of mine;
Yet always when I look death in the face,
When I clamber to the heights of sleep,
Or when I grow excited with wine,
Suddenly I meet your face.

PRESENCES

This night has been so strange that it seemed
As if the hair stood up on my head.
From going-down of the sun I have dreamed
That women laughing, or timid or wild,
In rustle of lace or silken stuff,
Climbed up my creaking stair. They had read
All I had rhymed of that monstrous thing
Returned and yet unrequited love.
They stood in the door and stood between
My great wood lecturn and the fire
Till I could hear their hearts beating:
One is a harlot, and one a child
That never looked upon man with desire,
And one it may be a queen.

THE BALLOON OF THE MIND

Hands, do what you're bid;
Bring the balloon of the mind
That bellies and drags in the wind
Into its narrow shed.

TO A SQUIRREL AT KYLE-NA-GNO

Come play with me;
Why should you run
Through the shaking tree
As though I'd a gun
To strike you dead?
When all I would do
Is to scratch your head
And let you go.

ON BEING ASKED FOR A WAR POEM

I think it better that in times like these
A poet keep his mouth shut, for in truth
We have no gift to set a statesman right;
He has had enough of meddling who can please
A young girl in the indolence of her youth,
Or an old man upon a winter's night.

IN MEMORY OF ALFRED POLLEXFEN

Five-and-twenty years have gone
Since old William Pollexfen
Laid his strong bones down in death
By his wife Elizabeth
In the grey stone tomb he made.
And after twenty years they laid
In that tomb by him and her,
His son George, the astrologer;
And Masons drove from miles away
To scatter the Acacia spray
Upon a melancholy man
Who had ended where his breath began.
Many a son and daughter lies
Far from the customary skies,
The Mall and Eades's grammar school,
In London or in Liverpool;
But where is laid the sailor John?
That so many lands had known:
Quiet lands or unquiet seas
Where the Indians trade or Japanese.
He never found his rest ashore,
Moping for one voyage more.
Where have they laid the sailor John?
And yesterday the youngest son,
A humorous, unambitious man,

Was buried near the astrologer;
And are we now in the tenth year?
Since he, who had been contented long,
A nobody in a great throng,
Decided he would journey home,
Now that his fiftieth year had come,
And "Mr. Alfred" be again
Upon the lips of common men
Who carried in their memory
His childhood and his family.
At all these death-beds women heard
A visionary white sea-bird
Lamenting that a man should die;
And with that cry I have raised my cry.

UPON A DYING LADY

I

HER COURTESY

With the old kindness, the old distinguished grace
She lies, her lovely piteous head amid dull red hair
Propped upon pillows, rouge on the pallor of her face.
She would not have us sad because she is lying there,
And when she meets our gaze her eyes are laughter-lit,
Her speech a wicked tale that we may vie with her
Matching our broken-hearted wit against her wit,
Thinking of saints and of Petronius Arbiter.

II

CERTAIN ARTISTS BRING HER DOLLS AND DRAWINGS

Bring where our Beauty lies
A new modelled doll, or drawing,
With a friend's or an enemy's

Features, or maybe showing
Her features when a tress
Of dull red hair was flowing
Over some silken dress
Cut in the Turkish fashion,
Or it may be like a boy's.
We have given the world our passion,
We have naught for death but toys.

III

SHE TURNS THE DOLLS' FACES TO THE WALL

Because to-day is some religious festival
They had a priest say Mass, and even the Japanese,
Heel up and weight on toe, must face the wall
— Pedant in passion, learned in old courtesies,
Vehement and witty she had seemed —; the Venetian lady
Who had seemed to glide to some intrigue in her red shoes,
Her domino, her panniered skirt copied from Longhi;
The meditative critic; all are on their toes,
Even our Beauty with her Turkish trousers on.
Because the priest must have like every dog his day
Or keep us all awake with baying at the moon,
We and our dolls being but the world were best away.

IV

THE END OF DAY

She is playing like a child
And penance is the play,
Fantastical and wild
Because the end of day
Shows her that some one soon
Will come from the house, and say —
Though play is but half-done —
"Come in and leave the play." —

V

HER RACE

She has not grown uncivil
As narrow natures would
And called the pleasures evil
Happier days thought good;
She knows herself a woman
No red and white of a face,
Or rank, raised from a common
Unreckonable race;
And how should her heart fail her
Or sickness break her will
With her dead brother's valour
For an example still.

VI

HER COURAGE

When her soul flies to the predestined dancing-place
(I have no speech but symbol, the pagan speech I made
Amid the dreams of youth) let her come face to face,
Amid that first astonishment, with Grania's shade
All but the terrors of the woodland flight forgot
That made her Dermuid dear, and some old cardinal
Pacing with half-closed eyelids in a sunny spot
Who had murmured of Giorgione at his latest breath —
Aye and Achilles, Timor, Babar, Barhaim, all
Who have lived in joy and laughed into the face of Death.

VII

HER FRIENDS BRING HER A CHRISTMAS TREE

Pardon, great enemy,
Without an angry thought
We've carried in our tree,

And here and there have bought
Till all the boughs are gay,
And she may look from the bed
On pretty things that may
Please a fantastic head.
Give her a little grace,
What if a laughing eye
Have looked into your face —
It is about to die.

EGO DOMINUS TUUS

HIC

On the grey sand beside the shallow stream
Under your old wind-beaten tower, where still
A lamp burns on beside the open book
That Michael Robartes left, you walk in the moon
And though you have passed the best of life still trace
Enthralled by the unconquerable delusion
Magical shapes.

ILLE

   By the help of an image
I call to my own opposite, summon all
That I have handled least, least looked upon.

HIC

And I would find myself and not an image.

ILLE

That is our modern hope and by its light
We have lit upon the gentle, sensitive mind
And lost the old nonchalance of the hand;

Whether we have chosen chisel, pen or brush
We are but critics, or but half create,
Timid, entangled, empty and abashed
Lacking the countenance of our friends.

HIC

                        And yet
The chief imagination of Christendom
Dante Alighieri so utterly found himself
That he has made that hollow face of his
More plain to the mind's eye than any face
But that of Christ.

ILLE

                        And did he find himself
Or was the hunger that had made it hollow
A hunger for the apple on the bough
Most out of reach? and is that spectral image
The man that Lapo and that Guido knew?
I think he fashioned from his opposite
An image that might have been a stony face,
Staring upon a bedouin's horse-hair roof
From doored and windowed cliff, or half upturned
Among the coarse grass and the camel dung.
He set his chisel to the hardest stone.
Being mocked by Guido for his lecherous life,
Derided and deriding, driven out
To climb that stair and eat that bitter bread,
He found the unpersuadable justice, he found
The most exalted lady loved by a man.

HIC

Yet surely there are men who have made their art
Out of no tragic war, lovers of life,
Impulsive men that look for happiness
And sing when they have found it.

ILLE

                    No, not sing,
For those that love the world serve it in action,
Grow rich, popular and full of influence,
And should they paint or write still it is action:
The struggle of the fly in marmalade.
The rhetorician would deceive his neighbours,
The sentimentalist himself; while art
Is but a vision of reality.
What portion in the world can the artist have
Who has awakened from the common dream
But dissipation and despair?

HIC

                    And yet
No one denies to Keats love of the world;
Remember his deliberate happiness.

ILLE

His art is happy but who knows his mind?
I see a schoolboy when I think of him,
With face and nose pressed to a sweet-shop window,
For certainly he sank into his grave
His senses and his heart unsatisfied,
And made — being poor, ailing and ignorant,
Shut out from all the luxury of the world,
The coarse-bred son of a livery stable-keeper —
Luxuriant song.

HIC

                    Why should you leave the lamp
Burning alone beside an open book,
And trace these characters upon the sands?
A style is found by sedentary toil
And by the imitation of great masters.

ILLE

Because I seek an image, not a book.
Those men that in their writings are most wise
Own nothing but their blind, stupefied hearts.
I call to the mysterious one who yet
Shall walk the wet sands by the edge of the stream
And look most like me, being indeed my double,
And prove of all imaginable things
The most unlike, being my anti-self,
And standing by these characters disclose
All that I seek; and whisper it as though
He were afraid the birds, who cry aloud
Their momentary cries before it is dawn,
Would carry it away to blasphemous men.

A PRAYER ON GOING INTO MY HOUSE

God grant a blessing on this tower and cottage
And on my heirs, if all remain unspoiled,
No table, or chair or stool not simple enough
For shepherd lads in Galilee; and grant
That I myself for portions of the year
May handle nothing and set eyes on nothing
But what the great and passionate have used
Throughout so many varying centuries.
We take it for the norm; yet should I dream
Sinbad the sailor's brought a painted chest,
Or image, from beyond the Loadstone Mountain,
That dream is a norm; and should some limb of the devil
Destroy the view by cutting down an ash
That shades the road, or setting up a cottage
Planned in a government office, shorten his life,
Manacle his soul upon the Red Sea bottom.

THE PHASES OF THE MOON

An old man cocked his ear upon a bridge;
He and his friend, their faces to the South,
Had trod the uneven road. Their boots were soiled,
Their Connemara cloth worn out of shape;
They had kept a steady pace as though their beds,
Despite a dwindling and late risen moon,
Were distant. An old man cocked his ear.

AHERNE

What made that sound?

ROBARTES

                    A rat or water-hen
Splashed, or an otter slid into the stream.
We are on the bridge; that shadow is the tower,
And the light proves that he is reading still.
He has found, after the manner of his kind,
Mere images; chosen this place to live in
Because, it may be, of the candle light
From the far tower where Milton's platonist
Sat late, or Shelley's visionary prince:
The lonely light that Samuel Palmer engraved,
An image of mysterious wisdom won by toil;
And now he seeks in book or manuscript
What he shall never find.

AHERNE

                    Why should not you
Who know it all ring at his door, and speak
Just truth enough to show that his whole life
Will scarcely find for him a broken crust
Of all those truths that are your daily bread;
And when you have spoken take the roads again?

ROBARTES

He wrote of me in that extravagant style
He had learnt from Pater, and to round his tale
Said I was dead; and dead I choose to be.

AHERNE

Sing me the changes of the moon once more;
True song, though speech: "mine author sung it me."

ROBARTES

Twenty-and-eight the phases of the moon,
The full and the moon's dark and all the crescents,
Twenty-and-eight, and yet but six-and-twenty
The cradles that a man must needs be rocked in:
For there's no human life at the full or the dark.
 From the first crescent to the half, the dream
 But summons to adventure and the man
 Is always happy like a bird or a beast;
 But while the moon is rounding towards the full
 He follows whatever whim's most difficult
 Among whims not impossible, and though scarred,
 As with the cat-o'-nine-tails of the mind,
 His body moulded from within his body
 Grows comelier. Eleven pass, and then
 Athenae takes Achilles by the hair,
 Hector is in the dust, Nietzsche is born,
 Because the heroes' crescent is the twelfth.
 And yet, twice born, twice buried, grow he must,
 Before the full moon, helpless as a worm.
 The thirteenth moon but sets the soul at war
 In its own being, and when that war's begun
 There is no muscle in the arm; and after
 Under the frenzy of the fourteenth moon
 The soul begins to tremble into stillness,
 To die into the labyrinth of itself!

AHERNE

Sing out the song; sing to the end, and sing
The strange reward of all that discipline.

ROBARTES

All thought becomes an image and the soul
Becomes a body: that body and that soul
Too perfect at the full to lie in a cradle,
Too lonely for the traffic of the world:
Body and soul cast out and cast away
Beyond the visible world.

AHERNE

                    All dreams of the soul
End in a beautiful man's or woman's body.

ROBARTES

Have you not always known it?

AHERNE

                    The song will have it
That those that we have loved got their long fingers
From death, and wounds, or on Sinai's top,
Or from some bloody whip in their own hands.
They ran from cradle to cradle till at last
Their beauty dropped out of the loneliness
Of body and soul.

ROBARTES

The lovers' heart knows that.

AHERNE

It must be that the terror in their eyes
Is memory or foreknowledge of the hour
When all is fed with light and heaven is bare.

ROBARTES

When the moon's full those creatures of the full
Are met on the waste hills by country men
Who shudder and hurry by: body and soul
Estranged amid the strangeness of themselves,
Caught up in contemplation, the mind's eye
Fixed upon images that once were thought,
For separate, perfect, and immovable
Images can break the solitude
Of lovely, satisfied, indifferent eyes.

And thereupon with aged, high-pitched voice
Aherne laughed, thinking of the man within,
His sleepless candle and laborious pen.

ROBARTES

And after that the crumbling of the moon.
The soul remembering its loneliness
Shudders in many cradles; all is changed,
It would be the world's servant, and as it serves,
Choosing whatever task's most difficult
Among tasks not impossible, it takes
Upon the body and upon the soul
The coarseness of the drudge.

AHERNE

Before the full
It sought itself and afterwards the world.

ROBARTES

Because you are forgotten, half out of life,
And never wrote a book your thought is clear.
Reformer, merchant, statesman, learned man,
Dutiful husband, honest wife by turn,
Cradle upon cradle, and all in flight and all
Deformed because there is no deformity
But saves us from a dream.

AHERNE

                    And what of those
That the last servile crescent has set free?

ROBARTES

Because all dark, like those that are all light,
They are cast beyond the verge, and in a cloud,
Crying to one another like the bats;
And having no desire they cannot tell
What's good or bad, or what it is to triumph
At the perfection of one's own obedience;
And yet they speak what's blown into the mind;
Deformed beyond deformity, unformed,
Insipid as the dough before it is baked,
They change their bodies at a word.

AHERNE

                              And then?

ROBARTES

When all the dough has been so kneaded up
That it can take what form cook Nature fancy
The first thin crescent is wheeled round once more.

AHERNE

But the escape; the song's not finished yet.

ROBARTES

Hunchback and saint and fool are the last crescents.
The burning bow that once could shoot an arrow
Out of the up and down, the wagon wheel
Of beauty's cruelty and wisdom's chatter —
Out of that raving tide — is drawn betwixt
Deformity of body and of mind.

AHERNE

Were not our beds far off I'd ring the bell,
Stand under the rough roof-timbers of the hall
Beside the castle door, where all is stark
Austerity, a place set out for wisdom
That he will never find; I'd play a part;
He would never know me after all these years
But take me for some drunken country man;
I'd stand and mutter there until he caught
"Hunchback and saint and fool," and that they came
Under the three last crescents of the moon,
And then I'd stagger out. He'd crack his wits
Day after day, yet never find the meaning.

And then he laughed to think that what seemed hard
Should be so simple — a bat rose from the hazels
And circled round him with its squeaky cry,
The light in the tower window was put out.

THE CAT AND THE MOON

The cat went here and there
And the moon spun round like a top,
And the nearest kin of the moon
The creeping cat looked up.
Black Minnaloushe stared at the moon,
For wander and wail as he would
The pure cold light in the sky
Troubled his animal blood.
Minnaloushe runs in the grass
Lifting his delicate feet.
Do you dance, Minnaloushe, do you dance?
When two close kindred meet
What better than call a dance,
Maybe the moon may learn,
Tired of that courtly fashion,
A new dance turn.
Minnaloushe creeps through the grass
From moonlit place to place,
The sacred moon overhead
Has taken a new phase.
Does Minnaloushe know that his pupils
Will pass from change to change,
And that from round to crescent,
From crescent to round they range?
Minnaloushe creeps through the grass
Alone, important and wise,
And lifts to the changing moon
His changing eyes.

THE SAINT AND THE HUNCHBACK

HUNCHBACK

Stand up and lift your hand and bless
A man that finds great bitterness
In thinking of his lost renown.
A Roman Caesar is held down
Under this hump.

SAINT

God tries each man
According to a different plan.
I shall not cease to bless because
I lay about me with the taws
That night and morning I may thrash
Greek Alexander from my flesh,
Augustus Caesar, and after these
That great rogue Alcibiades.

HUNCHBACK

To all that in your flesh have stood
And blessed, I give my gratitude,
Honoured by all in their degrees,
But most to Alcibiades.

TWO SONGS OF A FOOL

I

A speckled cat and a tame hare
Eat at my hearthstone
And sleep there;
And both look up to me alone
For learning and defence
As I look up to Providence.

I start out of my sleep to think
Some day I may forget
Their food and drink;
Or, the house door left unshut,
The hare may run till it's found
The horn's sweet note and the tooth of the hound.

I bear a burden that might well try
Men that do all by rule,
And what can I
That am a wandering witted fool
But pray to God that He ease
My great responsibilities.

II

I slept on my three-legged stool by the fire,
The speckled cat slept on my knee;
We never thought to enquire
Where the brown hare might be,
And whether the door were shut.
Who knows how she drank the wind
Stretched up on two legs from the mat,
Before she had settled her mind
To drum with her heel and to leap:
Had I but awakened from sleep
And called her name she had heard,

It may be, and had not stirred,
That now, it may be, has found
The horn's sweet note and the tooth of the hound.

ANOTHER SONG OF A FOOL

This great purple butterfly,
In the prison of my hands,
Has a learning in his eye
Not a poor fool understands.

Once he lived a schoolmaster
With a stark, denying look,
A string of scholars went in fear
Of his great birch and his great book.

Like the clangour of a bell,
Sweet and harsh, harsh and sweet,
That is how he learnt so well
To take the roses for his meat.

THE DOUBLE VISION OF MICHAEL ROBARTES

I

On the grey rock of Cashel the mind's eye
Has called up the cold spirits that are born
When the old moon is vanished from the sky
And the new still hides her horn.

Under blank eyes and fingers never still
The particular is pounded till it is man,
When had I my own will?
Oh, not since life began.

Constrained, arraigned, baffled, bent and unbent
By these wire-jointed jaws and limbs of wood,
Themselves obedient,
Knowing not evil and good;

Obedient to some hidden magical breath.
They do not even feel, so abstract are they,
So dead beyond our death,
Triumph that we obey.

II

On the grey rock of Cashel I suddenly saw
A Sphinx with woman breast and lion paw,
A Buddha, hand at rest,
Hand lifted up that blest;

And right between these two a girl at play
That it may be had danced her life away,
For now being dead it seemed
That she of dancing dreamed.

Although I saw it all in the mind's eye
There can be nothing solider till I die;
I saw by the moon's light
Now at its fifteenth night.

One lashed her tail; her eyes lit by the moon
Gazed upon all things known, all things unknown,
In triumph of intellect
With motionless head erect.

That other's moonlit eyeballs never moved,
Being fixed on all things loved, all things unloved,
Yet little peace he had
For those that love are sad.

Oh, little did they care who danced between,
And little she by whom her dance was seen

So that she danced. No thought,
Body perfection brought,

For what but eye and ear silence the mind
With the minute particulars of mankind?
Mind moved yet seemed to stop
As 'twere a spinning-top.

In contemplation had those three so wrought
Upon a moment, and so stretched it out
That they, time overthrown,
Were dead yet flesh and bone.

III

I knew that I had seen, had seen at last
That girl my unremembering nights hold fast
Or else my dreams that fly,
If I should rub an eye,

And yet in flying fling into my meat
A crazy juice that makes the pulses beat
As though I had been undone
By Homer's Paragon

Who never gave the burning town a thought;
To such a pitch of folly I am brought,
Being caught between the pull
Of the dark moon and the full,

The commonness of thought and images
That have the frenzy of our western seas.
Thereon I made my moan,
And after kissed a stone,

And after that arranged it in a song
Seeing that I, ignorant for so long,
Had been rewarded thus
In Cormac's ruined house.

MICHAEL ROBARTES AND THE DANCER

HE

Opinion is not worth a rush;
In this altar-piece the knight,
Who grips his long spear so to push
That dragon through the fading light,
Loved the lady; and it's plain
The half-dead dragon was her thought,
That every morning rose again
And dug its claws and shrieked and fought.
Could the impossible come to pass
She would have time to turn her eyes,
Her lover thought, upon the glass
And on the instant would grow wise.

SHE

You mean they argued.

HE

                  Put it so;
But bear in mind your lover's wage
Is what your looking-glass can show,
And that he will turn green with rage
At all that is not pictured there.

SHE

May I not put myself to college?

HE

Go pluck Athena by the hair;
For what mere book can grant a knowledge
With an impassioned gravity

Appropriate to that beating breast,
That vigorous thigh, that dreaming eye?
And may the devil take the rest.

SHE

And must no beautiful woman be
Learned like a man?

HE

　　　　　　　Paul Veronese
And all his sacred company
Imagined bodies all their days
By the lagoon you love so much,
For proud, soft, ceremonious proof
That all must come to sight and touch;
While Michael Angelo's Sistine roof
His "Morning" and his "Night" disclose
How sinew that has been pulled tight,
Or it may be loosened in repose,
Can rule by supernatural right
Yet be but sinew.

SHE

　　　　　　　I have heard said
There is great danger in the body.

HE

Did God in portioning wine and bread
Give man His thought or His mere body?

SHE

My wretched dragon is perplexed.

HE

I have principles to prove me right.
It follows from this Latin text
That blest souls are not composite,
And that all beautiful women may
Live in uncomposite blessedness,
And lead us to the like — if they
Will banish every thought, unless
The lineaments that please their view
When the long looking-glass is full,
Even from the foot-sole think it too.

SHE

They say such different things at school.

SOLOMON AND THE WITCH

And thus declared that Arab lady:
"Last night, where under the wild moon
On grassy mattress I had laid me,
Within my arms great Solomon,
I suddenly cried out in a strange tongue
Not his, not mine."
                        And he that knew
All sounds by bird or angel sung
Answered: "A crested cockerel crew
Upon a blossoming apple bough
Three hundred years before the Fall,
And never crew again till now,
And would not now but that he thought,
Chance being at one with Choice at last,
All that the brigand apple brought
And this foul world were dead at last.
He that crowed out eternity
Thought to have crowed it in again.

A lover with a spider's eye
Will find out some appropriate pain,
Aye, though all passion's in the glance,
For every nerve: lover tests lover
With cruelties of Choice and Chance;
And when at last that murder's over
Maybe the bride-bed brings despair
For each an imagined image brings
And finds a real image there;
Yet the world ends when these two things,
Though several, are a single light,
When oil and wick are burned in one;
Therefore a blessed moon last night
Gave Sheba to her Solomon."

"Yet the world stays":
                              "If that be so,
Your cockerel found us in the wrong
Although he thought it worth a crow.
Maybe an image is too strong
Or maybe is not strong enough."

"The night has fallen; not a sound
In the forbidden sacred grove
Unless a petal hit the ground,
Nor any human sight within it
But the crushed grass where we have lain;
And the moon is wilder every minute.
Oh, Solomon! let us try again."

AN IMAGE FROM A PAST LIFE

HE

Never until this night have I been stirred.
The elaborate star-light throws a reflection
On the dark stream,

Till all the eddies gleam;
And thereupon there comes that scream
From terrified, invisible beast or bird:
Image of poignant recollection.

SHE

An image of my heart that is smitten through
Out of all likelihood, or reason,
And when at last,
Youth's bitterness being past,
I had thought that all my days were cast
Amid most lovely places; smitten as though
It had not learned its lesson.

HE

Why have you laid your hands upon my eyes?
What can have suddenly alarmed you
Whereon 'twere best
My eyes should never rest?
What is there but the slowly fading west,
The river imaging the flashing skies,
All that to this moment charmed you?

SHE

A sweetheart from another life floats there
As though she had been forced to linger
From vague distress
Or arrogant loveliness,
Merely to loosen out a tress
Among the starry eddies of her hair
Upon the paleness of a finger.

HE

But why should you grow suddenly afraid
And start — I at your shoulder —

Imagining
That any night could bring
An image up, or anything
Even to eyes that beauty had driven mad,
But images to make me fonder.

SHE

Now she has thrown her arms above her head;
Whether she threw them up to flout me,
Or but to find,
Now that no fingers bind,
That her hair streams upon the wind,
I do not know, that know I am afraid
Of the hovering thing night brought me.

UNDER SATURN

Do not because this day I have grown saturnine
Imagine that lost love, inseparable from my thought
Because I have no other youth, can make me pine;
For how should I forget the wisdom that you brought,
The comfort that you made? Although my wits have gone
On a fantastic ride, my horse's flanks are spurred
By childish memories of an old cross Pollexfen,
And of a Middleton, whose name you never heard,
And of a red-haired Yeats whose looks, although he died
Before my time, seem like a vivid memory.
You heard that labouring man who had served my people.
    He said
Upon the open road, near to the Sligo quay —
No, no, not said, but cried it out — "You have come again
And surely after twenty years it was time to come."
I am thinking of a child's vow sworn in vain
Never to leave that valley his fathers called their home.

November 1919

EASTER 1916

I have met them at close of day
Coming with vivid faces
From counter or desk among grey
Eighteenth-century houses.
I have passed with a nod of the head
Or polite meaningless words,
Or have lingered awhile and said
Polite meaningless words,
And thought before I had done
Of a mocking tale or a gibe
To please a companion
Around the fire at the club,
Being certain that they and I
But lived where motley is worn:
All changed, changed utterly:
A terrible beauty is born.

That woman's days were spent
In ignorant good will,
Her nights in argument
Until her voice grew shrill.
What voice more sweet than hers
When young and beautiful,
She rode to harriers?
This man had kept a school
And rode our winged horse;
This other his helper and friend
Was coming into his force;
He might have won fame in the end,
So sensitive his nature seemed,
So daring and sweet his thought.
This other man I had dreamed
A drunken, vain-glorious lout.
He had done most bitter wrong
To some who are near my heart,
Yet I number him in the song;

He, too, has resigned his part
In the casual comedy;
He, too, has been changed in his turn,
Transformed utterly:
A terrible beauty is born.

Hearts with one purpose alone
Through summer and winter seem
Enchanted to a stone
To trouble the living stream.
The horse that comes from the road,
The rider, the birds that range
From cloud to tumbling cloud,
Minute by minute they change;
A shadow of cloud on the stream
Changes minute by minute;
A horse-hoof slides on the brim,
And a horse plashes within it
Where long-legged moor-hens dive,
And hens to moor-cocks call.
Minute by minute they live:
The stone's in the midst of all.

Too long a sacrifice
Can make a stone of the heart.
O when may it suffice?
That is heaven's part, our part
To murmur name upon name,
As a mother names her child
When sleep at last has come
On limbs that had run wild.
What is it but nightfall?
No, no, not night but death;
Was it needless death after all?
For England may keep faith
For all that is done and said.
We know their dream; enough
To know they dreamed and are dead;
And what if excess of love

Bewildered them till they died?
I write it out in a verse —
MacDonagh and MacBride
And Connolly and Pearse
Now and in time to be,
Wherever green is worn,
Are changed, changed utterly:
A terrible beauty is born.

September 25, 1916

SIXTEEN DEAD MEN

O but we talked at large before
The sixteen men were shot,
But who can talk of give and take,
What should be and what not
While those dead men are loitering there
To stir the boiling pot?

You say that we should still the land
Till Germany's overcome;
But who is there to argue that
Now Pearse is deaf and dumb?
And is their logic to outweigh
MacDonagh's bony thumb?

How could you dream they'd listen
That have an ear alone
For those new comrades they have found
Lord Edward and Wolfe Tone,
Or meddle with our give and take
That converse bone to bone?

THE ROSE TREE

"O words are lightly spoken,"
Said Pearse to Connolly,
"Maybe a breath of politic words
Has withered our Rose Tree;
Or maybe but a wind that blows
Across the bitter sea."

"It needs to be but watered,"
James Connolly replied,
"To make the green come out again
And spread on every side,
And shake the blossom from the bud
To be the garden's pride."

"But where can we draw water,"
Said Pearse to Connolly,
"When all the wells are parched away?
O plain as plain can be
There's nothing but our own red blood
Can make a right Rose Tree."

ON A POLITICAL PRISONER

She that but little patience knew,
From childhood on, had now so much
A grey gull lost its fear and flew
Down to her cell and there alit,
And there endured her fingers' touch
And from her fingers ate its bit.

Did she in touching that lone wing
Recall the years before her mind
Became a bitter, an abstract thing,
Her thought some popular enmity:

Blind and leader of the blind
Drinking the foul ditch where they lie?

When long ago I saw her ride
Under Ben Bulben to the meet,
The beauty of her country-side
With all youth's lonely wildness stirred,
She seemed to have grown clean and sweet
Like any rock-bred, sea-borne bird:

Sea-borne, or balanced on the air
When first it sprang out of the nest
Upon some lofty rock to stare
Upon the cloudy canopy,
While under its storm-beaten breast
Cried out the hollows of the sea.

THE LEADERS OF THE CROWD

They must to keep their certainty accuse
All that are different of a base intent;
Pull down established honour; hawk for news
Whatever their loose phantasy invent
And murmur it with bated breath, as though
The abounding gutter had been Helicon
Or calumny a song. How can they know
Truth flourishes where the student's lamp has shone,
And there alone, that have no solitude?
So the crowd come they care not what may come.
They have loud music, hope every day renewed
And heartier loves; that lamp is from the tomb.

TOWARDS BREAK OF DAY

Was it the double of my dream
The woman that by me lay
Dreamed, or did we halve a dream
Under the first cold gleam of day?

I thought: "There is a waterfall
Upon Ben Bulben side,
That all my childhood counted dear;
Were I to travel far and wide
I could not find a thing so dear."
My memories had magnified
So many times childish delight.

I would have touched it like a child
But knew my finger could but have touched
Cold stone and water. I grew wild
Even accusing heaven because
It had set down among its laws:
Nothing that we love over-much
Is ponderable to our touch.

I dreamed towards break of day,
The cold blown spray in my nostril.
But she that beside me lay
Had watched in bitterer sleep
The marvellous stag of Arthur,
That lofty white stag, leap
From mountain steep to steep.

DEMON AND BEAST

For certain minutes at the least
That crafty demon and that loud beast
That plague me day and night
Ran out of my sight;
Though I had long pernned in the gyre,
Between my hatred and desire,
I saw my freedom won
And all laugh in the sun.

The glittering eyes in a death's head
Of old Luke Wadding's portrait said

Welcome, and the Ormonds all
Nodded upon the wall,
And even Stafford smiled as though
It made him happier to know
I understood his plan.
Now that the loud beast ran
There was no portrait in the Gallery
But beckoned to sweet company,
For all men's thoughts grew clear
Being dear as mine are dear.

But soon a tear-drop started up
For aimless joy had made me stop
Beside the little lake
To watch a white gull take
A bit of bread thrown up into the air;
Now gyring down and pernning there
He splashed where an absurd
Portly green-pated bird
Shook off the water from his back;
Being no more demoniac
A stupid happy creature
Could rouse my whole nature.

Yet I am certain as can be
That every natural victory
Belongs to beast or demon,
That never yet had freeman
Right mastery of natural things,
And that mere growing old, that brings
Chilled blood, this sweetness brought;
Yet have no dearer thought
Than that I may find out a way
To make it linger half a day.

O what a sweetness strayed
Through barren Thebaid,
Or by the Mareotic sea
When that exultant Anthony

And twice a thousand more
Starved upon the shore
And withered to a bag of bones:
What had the Caesars but their thrones?

THE SECOND COMING

Turning and turning in the widening gyre
The falcon cannot hear the falconer;
Things fall apart; the centre cannot hold;
Mere anarchy is loosed upon the world,
The blood-dimmed tide is loosed, and everywhere
The ceremony of innocence is drowned;
The best lack all conviction, while the worst
Are full of passionate intensity.

Surely some revelation is at hand;
Surely the Second Coming is at hand.
The Second Coming! Hardly are those words out
When a vast image out of *Spiritus Mundi*
Troubles my sight: somewhere in sands of the desert
A shape with lion body and the head of a man,
A gaze blank and pitiless as the sun,
Is moving its slow thighs, while all about it
Reel shadows of the indignant desert birds.
The darkness drops again; but now I know
That twenty centuries of stony sleep
Were vexed to nightmare by a rocking cradle,
And what rough beast, its hour come round at last,
Slouches towards Bethlehem to be born?

A PRAYER FOR MY DAUGHTER

Once more the storm is howling and half hid
Under this cradle-hood and coverlid
My child sleeps on. There is no obstacle
But Gregory's wood and one bare hill
Whereby the haystack and roof-levelling wind,
Bred on the Atlantic, can be stayed;
And for an hour I have walked and prayed
Because of the great gloom that is in my mind.

I have walked and prayed for this young child an hour
And heard the sea-wind scream upon the tower,
And under the arches of the bridge, and scream
In the elms above the flooded stream;
Imagining in excited reverie
That the future years had come,
Dancing to a frenzied drum,
Out of the murderous innocence of the sea.

May she be granted beauty and yet not
Beauty to make a stranger's eye distraught,
Or hers before a looking-glass, for such,
Being made beautiful overmuch,
Consider beauty a sufficient end,
Lose natural kindness and maybe
The heart-revealing intimacy
That chooses right and never find a friend.

Helen being chosen found life flat and dull
And later had much trouble from a fool,
While that great Queen, that rose out of the spray,
Being fatherless could have her way
Yet chose a bandy-legged smith for man.
It's certain that fine women eat
A crazy salad with their meat
Whereby the Horn of Plenty is undone.

In courtesy I'd have her chiefly learned;
Hearts are not had as a gift but hearts are earned
By those that are not entirely beautiful;
Yet many, that have played the fool
For beauty's very self, has charm made wise,
And many a poor man that has roved,
Loved and thought himself beloved,
From a glad kindness cannot take his eyes.

May she become a flourishing hidden tree
That all her thoughts may like the linnet be,
And have no business but dispensing round
Their magnanimities of sound,
Nor but in merriment begin a chase,
Nor but in merriment a quarrel.
Oh, may she live like some green laurel
Rooted in one dear perpetual place.

My mind, because the minds that I have loved,
The sort of beauty that I have approved,
Prosper but little, has dried up of late,
Yet knows that to be choked with hate
May well be of all evil chances chief.
If there's no hatred in a mind
Assault and battery of the wind
Can never tear the linnet from the leaf.

An intellectual hatred is the worst,
So let her think opinions are accursed.
Have I not seen the loveliest woman born
Out of the mouth of Plenty's horn,
Because of her opinionated mind
Barter that horn and every good
By quiet natures understood
For an old bellows full of angry wind?

Considering that, all hatred driven hence,
The soul recovers radical innocence
And learns at last that it is self-delighting,

Self-appeasing, self-affrighting,
And that its own sweet will is heaven's will;
She can, though every face should scowl
And every windy quarter howl
Or every bellows burst, be happy still.

And may her bride-groom bring her to a house
Where all's accustomed, ceremonious;
For arrogance and hatred are the wares
Peddled in the thoroughfares.
How but in custom and in ceremony
Are innocence and beauty born?
Ceremony's a name for the rich horn,
And custom for the spreading laurel tree.

June 1919

A MEDITATION IN TIME OF WAR

For one throb of the Artery,
While on that old grey stone I sat
Under the old wind-broken tree,
I knew that One is animate
Mankind inanimate phantasy.

TO BE CARVED ON A STONE AT THOOR BALLYLEE

I, the poet William Yeats,
With old mill boards and sea-green slates,
And smithy work from the Gort forge,
Restored this tower for my wife George;
And may these characters remain
When all is ruin once again.

Alphabetical List of Titles
and First Lines

DOVER · THRIFT · EDITIONS

All books complete and unabridged. All 5³⁄₁₆ x 8¹⁄₄, paperbound.
Just $1.00—$2.00 in U.S.A.

A selection of the more than 200 titles in the series.

FLATLAND: A ROMANCE OF MANY DIMENSIONS, Edwin A. Abbott. 96pp. 27263-X $1.00

WINESBURG, OHIO, Sherwood Anderson. 160pp. 28269-4 $2.00

PRIDE AND PREJUDICE, Jane Austen. 272pp. 28473-5 $2.00

SENSE AND SENSIBILITY, Jane Austen. 272pp. 29049-2 $2.00

CIVIL WAR STORIES, Ambrose Bierce. 128pp. 28038-1 $1.00

THE DEVIL'S DICTIONARY, Ambrose Bierce. 144pp. 27542-6 $1.00

SONGS OF INNOCENCE AND SONGS OF EXPERIENCE, William Blake. 64pp. 27051-3 $1.00

THE CLASSIC TRADITION OF HAIKU: An Anthology, Faubion Bowers (ed.). 96pp. 29274-6 $1.50

SONNETS FROM THE PORTUGUESE AND OTHER POEMS, Elizabeth Barrett Browning. 64pp. 27052-1 $1.00

MY LAST DUCHESS AND OTHER POEMS, Robert Browning. 128pp. 27783-6 $1.00

SELECTED POEMS, George Gordon, Lord Byron. 112pp. 27784-4 $1.00

ALICE'S ADVENTURES IN WONDERLAND, Lewis Carroll. 96pp. 27543-4 $1.00

O PIONEERS!, Willa Cather. 128pp. 27785-2 $1.00

THE CHERRY ORCHARD, Anton Chekhov. 64pp. 26682-6 $1.00

THE AWAKENING, Kate Chopin. 128pp. 27786-0 $1.00

THE RIME OF THE ANCIENT MARINER AND OTHER POEMS, Samuel Taylor Coleridge. 80pp. 27266-4 $1.00

THE ANALECTS, Confucius. 128pp. 28484-0 $2.00

HEART OF DARKNESS, Joseph Conrad. 80pp. 26464-5 $1.00

THE RED BADGE OF COURAGE, Stephen Crane. 112pp. 26465-3 $1.00

MOLL FLANDERS, Daniel Defoe. 256pp. 29093-X $2.00

A CHRISTMAS CAROL, Charles Dickens. 80pp. 26865-9 $1.00

SELECTED POEMS, Emily Dickinson. 64pp. 26466-1 $1.00

SELECTED POEMS, John Donne. 96pp. 27788-7 $1.00

NOTES FROM THE UNDERGROUND, Fyodor Dostoyevsky. 96pp. 27053-X $1.00

SIX GREAT SHERLOCK HOLMES STORIES, Sir Arthur Conan Doyle. 112pp. 27055-6 $1.00

THE SOULS OF BLACK FOLK, W. E. B. Du Bois. 176pp. 28041-1 $2.00

SILAS MARNER, George Eliot. 160pp. 29246-0 $1.50

THE CONCORD HYMN AND OTHER POEMS, Ralph Waldo Emerson. 64pp. 29059-X $1.00

MEDEA, Euripides. 64pp. 27548-5 $1.00

THE AUTOBIOGRAPHY OF BENJAMIN FRANKLIN, Benjamin Franklin. 144pp. 29073-5 $1.50

THIS SIDE OF PARADISE, F. Scott Fitzgerald. 208pp. 28999-0 $2.00

A BOY'S WILL AND NORTH OF BOSTON, Robert Frost. 112pp. (Available in U.S. only) 26866-7 $1.00

WHERE ANGELS FEAR TO TREAD, E. M. Forster. 128pp. (Available in U.S. only) 27791-7 $1.00

THE SCARLET LETTER, Nathaniel Hawthorne. 192pp. 28048-9 $2.00

A DOLL'S HOUSE, Henrik Ibsen. 80pp. 27062-9 $1.00

THE TURN OF THE SCREW, Henry James. 96pp. 26684-2 $1.00

VOLPONE, Ben Jonson. 112pp. 28049-7 $1.00

DUBLINERS, James Joyce. 160pp. 26870-5 $1.00

A PORTRAIT OF THE ARTIST AS A YOUNG MAN, James Joyce. 192pp. 28050-0 $2.00

THE METAMORPHOSIS AND OTHER STORIES, Franz Kafka. 92pp. 29030-1 $1.50